wisdom
Spiritual Insights from the Great Traditions

It is a notable feature of human life that in all cultures and in almost every part of the globe there have been men and women who have understood — as though from 'inside' — the origin and existence of things. The rest of us often call these clear-sighted people 'wise', and what they understand 'insights'.

Whatever time and circumstances such people are born into, what they say or write carries a common stamp, a natural authority and ease. Their statements sound true. The manner of their speech and the colour of their language and expression often vary greatly but what they say has a common character.

Perhaps by quietly contemplating these statements we can share something of their wisdom.

Is there not one true coin for which
all things ought to be exchanged?

And that is wisdom

PLATO

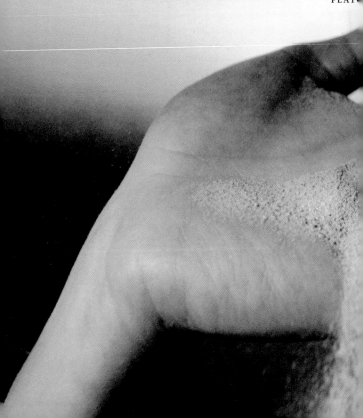

Whoever wants to meet God,

God wants to meet him

MUHAMMAD

The soul is not in the universe

On the contrary, the universe is in the Soul

PLOTINUS

If you go working with the

light available,

you will meet your Master,

as he himself

will be seeking you

SRI RAMANA MAHARSHI

You have slept for millions and
millions of years.
Why not wake up this morning?

KABIR

Wisdom is the principal thing;

therefore get wisdom

BIBLE

Each soul must meet the morning sun, the

new, sweet earth, and the Great Silence alone

OHIYESA

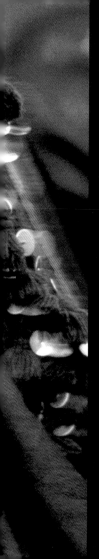

I saw my Lord

with the eye of my heart,

and I said,

'Who art Thou?'

He said,

'Thou'

BAYAZID OF BISTAM

It is only evil and ignorance

Truth and wisdom

that have many shapes.

are one and the same

ABBOT LEE LISAN

Seek

knowledge

from

the

cradle

to

the

grave

MUHAMMAD

If you want to be given everything,

give everything up

Don't pretend

        to know something

you haven't experienced

RUMI

To have but few desires

and to be satisfied with

simple things is the sign

of a superior person

GAMPOPA

God can never be found by seeking,

yet only seekers find Him

BAYAZID OF BISTAM

When a superior man
hears of the Way,
he immediately begins
to embody it.

When an average man
hears of the Way,
he half believes it,
half doubts it.

When a foolish man
hears of the Way,
he laughs out loud.

If he didn't laugh,
it wouldn't be the Way

TAO TE CHING

Worship God as if you see Him.

If you do not see Him,

know that He sees you

MUHAMMAD

Not that which goeth into the mouth

defileth a man;

but that which cometh out of the mouth,

this defileth a man

JESUS

There is as much

in the little space within

the heart as there is in

the whole world outside.

Heaven, earth, fire,

wind, sun, moon,

lightning, stars;

whatever is

and whatever is not,

everything is there

CHHANDOGYA UPANISHAD

To know and yet not to do is in fact not to know

WANG YANG MING

Thou must be emptied
of that wherewith thou art full,
that thou mayest be filled with that
whereof thou art empty

ST AUGUSTINE

The truly wise mourn for neither

he living nor the dead

BHAGAVAD GITA

Give up wanting what other people have

RUMI

Who are the learned? They who

practise what they know

MUHAMMAD

Silence is the garden of meditation

ALI

Who is wise?

He who learns from all

TALMUD

The greatest good for man

is to become conformable to

the will of God

ST THOMAS AQUINAS

All the Scriptures are meant only to make

man retrace his steps to the original source

SRI RAMANA MAHARSHI

wisdom

Published in England by

FOUR SEASONS
PUBLISHING

16 Orchard Rise, Kingston upon Thames, Surrey, KT2 7EY

Designed in association with
THE BRIDGEWATER BOOK COMPANY

Printed in Singapore

Editorial consultant: Philip Novak

*The publishers would like to thank the Gettyone Stone Picture Library,
The Image Bank and Corbis Images for the use of pictures*